ALLIGATORS

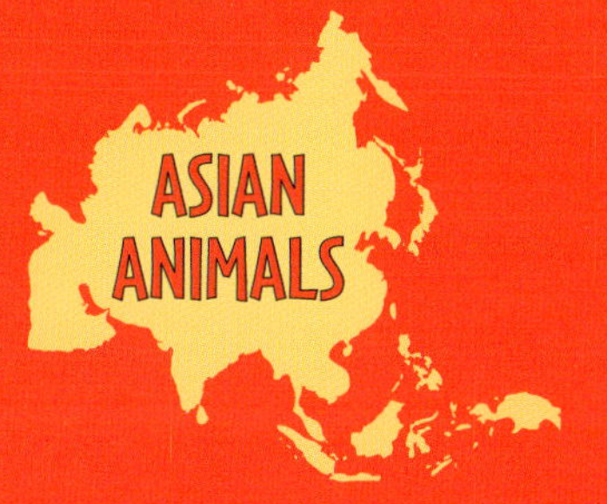

Alicia Rodriguez

TABLE OF CONTENTS

A Pelican Book

Teaching Tips for Caregivers and Teachers:

Research shows that one of the best ways for students to learn a new topic is to read about it.

Before Reading

- Read the title and predict what the book will be about.
- Read the "Words to Know" and discuss the meaning of each word.
- Read the back cover to see what the book is about.

During Reading

- When a student gets to a word that is unknown, ask them to look at the rest of the sentence to find clues to help with the meaning of the unknown word.
- Motivate students with praise and encouragement.

After Reading

- Discuss the main idea of the book.
- Ask students to give one detail that they learned in the book.

Sight Words

a	big	in	most
all	can	is	on
also	eat	land	they
an	four	live	this
and	have	long	water

Words to Know

alligator

feet

fish

snout

tail

teeth

This is an **alligator**.

alligator

All alligators have four **feet**.

foot

Most alligators have a long **snout**.

They also have a long **tail**.
tail

Alligators can live on land and in water.

Most alligators eat **fish**.

fish

All alligators have big **teeth**!

teeth

Index

Written by: Alicia Rodriguez
Design by: Under the Oaks Media
Series Development: James Earley
Editor: Kim Thompson

Photos: Shutterstock: Danny Ye: cover, p. 4-5; Piyathep: p7; Design Studio: p. 8; Trababazo Rivas: p. 9; meunierd: p. 10-11; Jamilah1444: p. 13; Pavel Filatov

Library of Congress PCN Data
Alligators / Alicia Rodriguez
Asian Animals
ISBN 978-1-63897-439-0(hard cover)
ISBN 978-1-63897-554-0(paperback)
ISBN 978-1-63897-669-1(EPUB)
ISBN 978-1-63897-784-1(eBook)
Library of Congress Control Number: 2022933724

Printed in the United States of America.

Seahorse Publishing Company
www.seahorsepub.com

Published in the United States
Seahorse Publishing
PO Box 771325
Coral Springs, FL 33077